AS ANGELS HOVER OVER

Inspired Writings
By
SANDRA J YEARMAN

SERAPHIM PUBLISHING LLC

WE WILL BRING LIGHT TO ALL THE DARK PLACES

Registered trademark-
Sandra J Yearman
Seraphim Publishing
438 Water St. Cambridge, WI 53523

Copyright © 2008 Sandra J Yearman
Produced in the United States of America
Author : Sandra J Yearman
Editor: Sandra J Yearman
Cover Design by Sandra J Yearman
Layout and design by Sandra J Yearman

All rights reserved. No part of this book may be reproduced, stored in or introduced into a retrieval system, or transmitted, in any form or by any means, electronic or mechanical, including photocopying or recording or otherwise copied for public or private use—other than for "fair use" as brief quotations embodied in articles and reviews—without written permission from the author.

Library of Congress Control Number: 2009907495
ISBN: 978-0-9841506-1-8
First Edition

Jesus Your Presence
Changed Our World
Your Foot Prints Will
Be Seen Through Eternity
Let Thy Will Be Done
Amen
Amen
Amen

CONTENTS

DEDICATION

As Angels Hover Over 7
A Gift From Heaven....................10
The Holy Lamb..........................12
Resurrection..............................14
As Angels Fly.............................16

SEEKING LIGHT IN THE DARKNESS

The Star That Took The Night................19
Help Me To Save This Creature.............21
At What Cost 24
Seek Guidance...27
Bring Us To Paradise 29
In This World I Wander.........................31
Lord Deliver Me From Darkness............34
Debt..36
Lord Give Me A Cord 38
God's Promise 39
Teach Us To Sing....................................41
The Fall..44
I Need To Remember..............................46
Lord Fill Us With Your Grace................48

CONTENTS

Goliath Will Always Be Before Us................50
Never Alone...52
This Child..54
Help Us To Heal..56
Awaken Within Us.......................................57
The Passing Of A Pet 59
I Will Kneel So I My Fly..............................61

COMING HOME

God Used A Star..64
The Song Of God..66
You Are The Living God.............................68
He Will Love Us Always..............................69
The Eyes Of Heaven....................................71
Bring Us Home..73
Amidst The Cries And Chaos 75
Walking With Angels 77

Dedication

As Angels Hover Over

As Angels hover over
Waiting for us to pray
To ask them to help us
And in our lives to stay

As Angels hover over
'Speak to us' They say
To carry and protect us
And to show us God's Holy Way

As Angels hover over
A tear they sometimes cry
Because we do not listen
And choose a path to die

As Angels hover over
Their presence we fear
We do not want to believe
That Holiness is near

As Angels hover over
And bless us every day
They show us love and mercy
And in our lives they stay

As Angels hover over
Their presence represents
The Love that God has for us
A Love that is Heaven sent

In their wings we cradle
In their love we heal
In their Holy presence
To our Holy God we should kneel

Our choices they destroy us
Our fears are in control
The darkness we call, defeats us
We are in danger of losing our souls

Yet God, His Love He shows us
His Mercy without end
Our sins He forgives us
And His Angels, He does send

Amen Amen Amen

A Gift From Heaven

God sent His blessings
To a dying world

His divine messenger to behold
The One of whom; the ancient
prophets had fore told

And the One who had created
Was not recognized

The Holy Gift from Heaven
Was rejected and despised

And man in their un-holiness
Glorified demons and their sins

They refused the Gift of Heaven
They refused to let Him in

They judged the Gift as humans
With darkness and with greed

They refused to listen
They refused the Holy seed

But God in all His Holiness
And Heaven with all its Might

Stood before a dying world
And darkness lost the fight

Amen Amen Amen

The Holy Lamb

Rejoice
In the Holy lamb
Rejoice
In the Son of God

Rejoice
In the Spirit of Heaven
Rejoice
In our redemption

Rejoice
In the Mercy of God the Father
Rejoice
In the Love of the Holy Son

Rejoice
In the miracles
Rejoice
In the Holy Three in One

Amen Amen Amen

Resurrection

The nectar of Heaven
His Holiness to see
He conquered our darkness
The Holy One in Three

Fulfilling God's promises
Taking our pain
Lighting the darkness
Our souls He did gain

Savior of many
Redeemer of all
His crucifixion
Was the dark one's great fall

Sent from His Father
Holy without blame
His blood cleansed our darkness
He came in God's Name

Amen Amen Amen

As Angels Fly

As Angels fly
On golden wings
The Song of God
Does Heaven sing

The Angels Song
The Holy dance
Choirs of Angels
Man's advance

Soaring through illusions
Transcending time
Worlds created
The Great I Am

Visions of Holiness
Prophets fore told
Dreams of creation
Angels of gold

Communion with Holiness
Release of our sins
Speaking with God
Return to where we begin

Amen Amen Amen

Seeking Light In The Darkness

The Star That Took The Night

God I lost a friend today
The sorrow is so great
I pray that You will keep her
For always, for her sake

A jewel she was in my life
A star that took the night
She taught me many lessons
My friend with Holy Sight

She always stood for justice
She forgave when she was wronged
She loved beyond all measure
She sang a Holy Song

She protected all around her
My teacher and my friend
Her presence will stay with me
Until the very end

God thank You for the blessing
She was in my life
You sent her at a time
When I was filled with strife

I teased that she had saved me
From a path that was not right
My friend who stood for justice
The star that took the night

Amen Amen Amen

Help Me To Save This Creature

God help me to save this creature
Who has been tortured by man's hand
The victims and neglected
It is time we took a stand

The Angels sing with Glory
As God watches from above
To stand before creation
With His Eternal Love

Darkness feeds on victims
The helpless and the weak
Too often we look away
Too often we do not speak

The Angels sing with Glory
As God watches from above
To stand before creation
With His Eternal Love

As the earth is eroded
As species are destroyed
As humans are murdered
Are we merely the demon's toys

The Angels sing with Glory
As God watches from above
To stand before creation
With His Eternal Love

God give us substance
God give us Grace
Remind us we are Your children
And that You blessed us in this place

Amen Amen Amen

At What Cost

What does it take for creation to stand against darkness
Why are we defined by our fears
Why is this world filled with victims
Do we make offerings of what we hold dear

If man is superior to the rest of creation
Because of the choices he can make
Then why is this planet dying
At what cost do we forsake

The majesty of creation
The life that we hold dear
The futures of our children
The freedoms we have here

At what point do we question our actions
When all the wildlife is gone
When the wilderness is barren
When the gardens are turned to stone

What worlds do we leave to our children
When man refuses to let go of his fear
Would he destroy all that is different
Will we remember only by our tears

God expose the demons among us
The altars built for unholy sacrifice
The fathers who would sell the children
Behind the death masks who would hide

God rain Your Fire in these dark worlds
Cleanse us of our fears
Cure us of this madness
Wipe away our tears

Amen Amen Amen

Seek Guidance

As we seek the answers
To life's mysteries
Pray to God for guidance
Pray that you will see

The answers that He sends you
No matter what their form
The signs He sends from Heaven
To guide you through the storm

And pray that you will listen
When whispers He does speak
His Voice to follow in the darkness
His Holiness to seek

Pray that He will help you
Distinguish among the masks
To follow the path of God
In His Holy Light to bask

Ask Him to protect you
From those who would corrupt your ways
Who would lead you into darkness
And death for all your days

Ask God to carry
You through the darkest night
Have faith in His Mercy
Have faith in His Might

Amen Amen Amen

Bring Us To Paradise

There are some who would applaud
the demons
In their unholy escapades
To destroy all that God has given
To destroy all that God has made

They look to take false glory
They look to steal the prize
They wear false masks
In their unholy guise

They prey upon the victims
They terrorize the meek
They are empowered
By the souls that they seek

God stand before Your children
Save us in these lives
Lift us from these dark worlds
Bring us to paradise

Amen Amen Amen

In This World I Wander

As I have wandered wearily
On this path of life
Tired and weakened
By this world of strife

As I have wandered wearily
Unnamed foes to behold
Searching for the riches
That mankind had fore told

As I have wandered wearily
My days as dark as night
My choices and ambitions
Blinded my earthly sight

All these years I have wandered
For earthly riches to behold
All these years I have wandered
As one is dead and one is cold

Lord my sight was narrow
And my heart was as stone
I gathered my earthly riches
But was still lost and still alone

Lord my eyes are open
And my sins You will Atone
Lord my heart is open
And now I have found my Home

All the riches of this world
Brought nothing of value to me
The treasures that I sought are small
In comparison to finding Thee

I am no longer weary
I am healed and I am whole
My life now has a purpose
My journey has a goal

Lord cleanse away my darkness
Fill me with Your Peace
Bless me with the Grace of God
Your Holy Light in me increase

Amen Amen Amen

Lord Deliver Me From Darkness

Lord deliver me from darkness
I am being swallowed by the choices I have made
My being is collapsing form the weight of my sins
I am falling

Lord help me
I am a voice screaming from the darkness
I am in so much pain
I am in so much confusion
I am dying

Lord please give me life
Lord please shine Your Face upon me
Lord please forgive me

Lord ignite Your Holy Flame
within me
Do not let the darkness extinguish my
light
Save me my Lord

Amen Amen Amen

Debt

Pay the debt to darkness
When you choose to sell your soul
There is no love and mercy
In the darkness that dwells below

People desire power
They fester with greed and hate
Desperate to feed their fears
They summon the darkest gate

They think that darkness
Can fulfill their earthly delights
Give them status and power
But there is a debt they owe the night

They do not understand
They do not realize
The answer to all their needs
Is right before their eyes

God is the only power
God is the only need
God will care and cradle
With His Holy speed

The choice is ours
And has always been
Do we choose freedom
Or the consequences of our sins

Amen Amen Amen

Lord Give Me A Cord

Lord give me a light in the darkness so
I know I am not alone
Lord give me a cord to cling to, until
You come for me
Lord give me a song for my soul to sing
Lord Help me to rise out of the
Darkness

Give me what I need to overcome my
fears, my sins
My un-holiness
Lord Bless me
Lord bring me Home

Amen Amen Amen

God's Promise

Through these worlds of darkness
The hells that we create

The mazes of fear and terror
Crippled by sin's heavy weight

The Lord has never left us
He is but a prayer away

Yet we cower in our prisons
In hell we choose to stay

To pray for God's Holy Light
Our sins would be exposed

Our darkness and our fears
As if Heaven does not already know

We can not hide from Heaven
We can not flee the Lord

Any shield that darkness has
Will be penetrated by the Holy Sword

Lord cleanse us from these dark worlds
Save us from our fate

Cut the chains that bind us
Bring us Home through
Gods' Holy Gate

Amen Amen Amen

Teach Us To Sing

There are those who spend their lives
Asking to see God's Face
Yet they are filled with darkness
Horror and disgrace

To use God for their dark agendas
His power to wield
The unholy will never touch Him
For God is creation's shield

There are those who spend their lives
Asking to hear God's Voice
But when He speaks
They do not listen, by their own choice

There are those who ask God to stand before them
But when He comes they hide and flee
They do not trust the Voice they hear inside their hearts
They do not trust what they see

God is with us always
He is never in disguise
He hears all our thoughts
He sees through our eyes

He knows our motivations
Our hopes and our fears
He is but a prayer away
Call out, He will hear

He carries us with His hands
He shelters us with His wings
He will teach us the Holy Song
We must ask Him to teach us to sing

Amen Amen Amen

The Fall

I stumbled through the darkness
The thickness of the wall
That I had built to bind me
To perpetuate the fall

I fell and no one listened
No one heard me call
Because the boundaries that we built
Perpetuated the fall

As I lay there dying
I was touched with Holy Grace
By an Angel who heard me crying
In the darkness of this place

Slowly I was lifted
For I fought with all my might
As much as I was suffering
I was still a child of the night

The Angel with His mercy
Held a mirror to me
But the darkness was so thick
My image, I could barely see

So the Heavens, lit the darkness
And I could hear some shriek with fear
As we saw our souls disfigured
In that Holy mirror

The Angel in His Mercy
Said 'God will hold you near'
'You see, He sees a different image'
'In that Holy mirror'

Amen Amen Amen

I Need To Remember

God when I am most troubled
When I am consumed with doubt
and fear
I need to remember
To call the Angels near

When I can no longer carry my
burdens
When I shriek with horror and pain
I need to remember
That I have All to gain

When I am being pulled into the
darkness
When I am weak and my soul cries
I need to remember
With You my healing lies

When I am weak from hunger
And my thirst is great
I need to remember
To enter the Holy Gate

Lord let Thy will be done

Amen Amen Amen

Lord Fill Us With Your Grace

God we beg of You to pardon us for
our sins
Lift us out of the darkness and into
Your Holy Light
Engulf us with Your Love
Guide us and protect us
Show us the path You would have
us take

Fill us with Your Grace
Help us to understand
Ignite within us the Flame of the
Holy Spirit
We surrender to Your Holiness

Let us dwell in the House of the Lord
Let the Lord dwell in our homes and in our hearts
Teach us, Lord, to pray
Help us to remember the Holiness in which we were created
Help us to see the Holiness in all of Your creations

God Bless us and carry us this day

Amen Amen Amen

Goliath Will Always Be Before Us

Goliath will always be before us
As long as we are of this world
As long as we are in these vessels

Goliath will always be before us
Trying to conquer
Trying to destroy
Spreading his terror

In a world long ago
Goliath was conquered and destroyed
By a boy with great faith

In all these worlds
And in all these ages
Faith has not lost its power

Lord give us the faith
To conquer the darkness

Lord give us the faith
To slay the monsters within us

Lord give us the faith
To destroy the demons who walk among us

Lord carry us

Amen Amen Amen

Never Alone

Abandoned by her family
Forsaken by her friends
Hopeless from the day they left
She thought it was the end

Taken to an abandoned house
Left there all alone
As fear was overtaking
God's Holy Light was shown

An Angel came up to her
And took her to her breast
And kissed her with the Love of God
At home she was at last

The Angel hovered over
And healed her with her love
And showered her with blessings
And gifts sent from above

The Angel never left her
She was never alone again
For God took her to His breast
And she returned from where she began

Amen Amen Amen

This Child

This is a child you would have thrown away
See how beautiful he is
See how holy he is

We are all God's family

How do we justify
Covering our eyes so that we do not see
Covering our ears so that we do not hear the cries
Allowing darkness to consume

How do we justify to our God that we stood by and allowed His creations to be destroyed

Do we say 'my Lord we were gripped with fear'
Do we say 'my Lord we were seized by ignorance'
Do we say 'my Lord we were filled with indifference'

Lord forgive us
Lord forgive us
Lord forgive us

And help us to see the Holiness You have created
In all of Your children

Lord save us all

Amen Amen Amen

Help Us To Heal

Help us Holy One to break
The patterns of abuse in our lives
The patterns of horror
The patterns of victimization

Help us to be stronger than our
addictions
Help us to overcome the monsters
within us
Help us to heal

Holy One forgive and cleanse us
And bring us back to the Light

Amen Amen Amen

Awaken Within Us

Thank You Lord for our bounty
And the blessings You give us daily
We do not thank You enough
We cloud our eyes with darkness
And do not see the beauty and
Holiness that is right before us

We do not see the Holiness in all of creation
We do not see the love
We do not see the care
We do not see the gifts
That You provide for us, as our Loving Father

Oh Lord, forgive us
And awaken within us
The Spirit of God

We seek dark thoughts
And actions to feel alive
Instead of aligning ourselves
With life itself

Oh Lord, forgive us
And awaken within us
The Spirit of God

Cleanse us and wash away the filth of
this world
Heal us
Bless us
And bring us Home

Oh Lord, forgive us
And awaken within us
The Spirit of God

Amen Amen Amen

The Passing Of A Pet

God I would ask for guidance
For a decision I must make
My life is filled with sadness
My heart is filled with ache

My pet, my friend, my family
Is preparing a journey to Thee
My loss is over whelming
My faith I turn to Thee

When do I assist him
On this path of life
I fear that he should suffer
His loss fills me with strife

I do not want to burden
The friend that stood by me
Help me to see through the tears
Help me, I ask of Thee

Give me the strength
To stay at his side
His love fills my heart
With You he will now abide

His memory will stay with me always
For love does not dissolve
If you can give him a message
Tell him, he will always have my love

Amen Amen Amen

I Will Kneel So I May Fly

As I wandered through these worlds
And darkness sought to steal
The Holiness within my soul
The illusions of what was real

Tempted and tormented
It is the human test
Breaking the chains of the damned
Is the salvation of the blessed

Lord strip me of my ego
Give me Holy Sight
Carry me in dark times
Protect me with Your Might

No matter what I gather
No matter what I gain
There is nothing so precious of this world
That I will put my soul in chains

Darkness has no power
I am not afraid to die
The Lord is my Shepherd
I will kneel so I may fly

Amen Amen Amen

Coming Home

God Used A Star

God used a brilliant star
To announce the birth of Jesus to this world

God used the glorious star
To announce He had fulfilled a promise

God used the light of the star
To show mankind the pathway Home

Jesus You are the Star sent from Heaven
You are the Promise fulfilled
You are the Pathway Home

Jesus You are the Light of our world
Your Holiness dissolves the darkness

To Your Glory

Amen Amen Amen

The Song Of God

The Teacher of Israel
The Song of God
The Light of the worlds
Stood before creation

His Presence here
Merged the worlds
For a moment in time
And we are blessed

His life brought Holiness
To our existence
His Light dissolved the darkness
And we are blessed

His Love forgave us
His Mercy healed us
His Courage saved us
And we are blessed

And we are blessed

Amen Amen Amen

You Are The Living God

You are the Living God
You are Life itself

You are the whisper in the wind
You are the sunshine in our worlds

You are the Song of our souls
You are the Way

You are the Light
You are the All

We believe
We love

Amen Amen Amen

He Will Love Us Always

Rejoice

God is in the house
His Presence will cleanse us
His Grace will heal us
His Power will protect us
We will be reborn in His Love

Sing praises

God is in the house
He will save us
He will transform us
He will bless us
He will restore us

Give thanks

God is in the house
He will remove the obstacles that
separate us
He will carry us Home
He will Love us always

Amen Amen Amen

The Eyes Of Heaven

The eyes of Heaven surround us
Friends often unseen to our eyes
Wings that hover over
Souls that hear us cry

Lights that God would send us
To guide us along the way
His Presence is always with us
His Spirit will always stay

Listen to the song your heart sings
Listen to the voice inside
Know the Angels hover
Know that God Abides

Pray that God will show you
How to see with Holy Sight
Ask to Hear His Voice
Pray to know His Might

Look for the signs from Heaven
They may come in any form
Do not close yourself to their presence
There will be light in every storm

The eyes of Heaven surround us
Friends often unseen to our eyes
Wings that hover over
Souls that hear us cry

Amen Amen Amen

Bring Us Home

Our Father, awaken within us the
Peace of God

Our Father, ignite within us the Spirit
of the Lord

Our Father, help us to remember what
we have long forgotten

Help us to remember the Song
Help us to remember our Holiness

Consume us with Your Grace
And bring Your children Home

Bring us Home
Bring us Home
In the arms of an Angel, bring us Home

Amen Amen Amen

Amidst The Cries And Chaos

Amidst the cries and chaos
The terror and the fear
The prayers that went to Heaven
As only God can hear

And from the mist came Angels
The army that God sent
To rescue all the victims
His promises, as meant

The demons focused on the light
And their victims did let go
As the warriors waged in battle
Their Holiness aglow

Angels in their Holiness
Stand before mankind
To save us from the darkness
To break the chains that bind

As darkness focused on the battle
The victims were set free
As a voice cried from the mist
'God, fill this world with Thee'

As this battle of creation
Still wages in our lives
Do we call out to the Heavens
Or choose a world to die

Amen Amen Amen

Walking With Angels

Walking with Angels
Invisible to see
Their presence is with us
Messengers from Thee

A whisper from Heaven
Miracles to behold
They guide and protect us
As Heaven fore told

Lighting our darkness
Teaching His Song
Instruments of God
Correcting our wrongs

In our hour of darkness
They draw us near
To comfort and guide us
And heal all our fears

And in the silence
Their whispers you will hear
A Heavenly reminder
That God is always near

Amen Amen Amen

As Angels Hover Over
Their Presence Represents
The Love That God Has For Us
A Love That Is Heaven Sent
Amen
Amen
Amen

www.ingramcontent.com/pod-product-compliance
Lightning Source LLC
Chambersburg PA
CBHW051712040426
42446CB00008B/844